MW00905758

Progress Tests

Maths

Steve Mills and Hilary Koll

Age 5–6
Year 1
Key Stage 1

Hachette UK's policy is to use papers that are natural, renewable and recyclable products and made from wood grown in sustainable forests. The logging and manufacturing processes are expected to conform to the environmental regulations of the country of origin.

Orders: please contact Bookpoint Ltd, 130 Milton Park, Abingdon, Oxon OX14 4SB. Telephone: (44) 01235 827720. Fax: (44) 01235 400454. Lines are open 9.00a.m.–5.00p.m., Monday to Saturday, with a 24-hour message answering service. Visit our website at www.hoddereducation.co.uk.

© Steve Mills and Hilary Koll 2013
First published in 2013 exclusively for WHSmith by
Hodder Education
An Hachette UK Company
338 Euston Road
London NW1 3BH

Impression number   10 9 8 7 6 5 4 3 2 1
Year   2018 2017 2016 2015 2014 2013

Cover illustration by Oxford Designers and Illustrators Ltd
Illustrations by Fakenham Prepress Solutions, Fakenham, Norfolk NR21 8NN
Typeset in 16pt Folio by Fakenham Prepress Solutions, Fakenham, Norfolk NR21 8NN
Printed in Great Britain by Hobbs the Printers Ltd, Totton, Hampshire SO40 3WX

A catalogue record for this title is available from the British Library.

ISBN: 978 1444 188 233

Introduction

How this book can help your child

This book contains practice of the essential areas of mathematics expected of children aged 5–6. Each of the Progress Tests covers a key area, including number work, measurement, shape and space work and data handling.

This book provides opportunity for testing children's knowledge, skills and understanding of these key areas. Regular practice helps children to build a good mathematical foundation and to gain confidence in all aspects of the curriculum.

How to use this book

To get the most from this book:
- Encourage your child to take the tests regularly, ideally one per day.
- Read the first question aloud in different ways e.g. use the words 'add, plus' etc. to help your child recognise what to do, e.g. whether to add, double or take away.
- Time each test. As your child becomes more confident, the time should decrease.
- If the early tests take more than 15 minutes to complete, suggest that your child tackles a section at a time with a break in-between.
- Involve your child in marking the tests and talk together about any incorrect answers. Be sensitive and draw more attention to those that were correct, asking your child to tell you how they tackled the question and what they found difficult about it.
- When the marks for the tests are added up, the results may be recorded on the record sheet (on the inside back cover). This will give you and the children a sense of how well they are doing.
- Draw attention to improvements made in the times or marks.
- Praise and encourage your child at all stages.

Tick the team that has **more** in each pair.

1  or

2  or

3  or

Tick the bowl that has **fewer** apples in each pair.

4  or

5  or

6  or

Mark your answers. How well did you do?

Mark ___6___ out of 6   Time taken _____

How many?

1  3

4 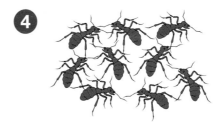 9

2  5

5  6

3  7

Put these numbers in order, smallest first.

6 5, 2, 8, 4   2, 4, 5, 8

7 2, 7, 6, 11   2, 6, 7, 11

8 6, 12, 9, 1   1, 6, 9, 12

9 14, 18, 13, 15   13, 14, 15, 18 18

Mark your answers. How well did you do?

Mark 9 out of 9   Time taken

5

Test 3: Numbers to 100

Write the missing numbers in each sequence.

1 1, 2, 3, 4, [5], 6, 7, …

2 4, 5, 6, 7, 8, [9], 10, 11, …

3 10, 11, 12, 13, 14, [15], 16, …

4 16, 17, [18], 19, 20, …

Count on in ones.

5 13, 14, 15, 16, [17], [18], [19]

6 30, 31, 32, 33, 34, [35], [36], [37]

7 95, 96, 97, 98, [99], [100], [101]

Count back in ones.

8 83, 82, 81, 80, [79], [78], [77]

9 64, 63, 62, 61, [60], [59], [58]

10 100, 99, 98, 97, [96], [95], [94]

Mark your answers. How well did you do?

Mark [10] out of 10   Time taken [   ]

Count in twos and fill in the missing numbers.

1 2, 4, 6, ☐, 10, 12, ☐, 16, …

2 2, ☐, 6, 8, 10, 12, 14, ☐, 18, 20, …

3 10, 12, 14, ☐, ☐, 20, 22, ☐, …

Count in fives and fill in the missing numbers.

4 5, 10, 15, 20, ☐, 30, 35, 40, ☐, …

5 5, ☐, 15, 20, 25, 30, 35, ☐, 45, 50, …

6 20, 25, 30, 35, 40, ☐, ☐, 55, ☐, …

Count in tens and fill in the missing numbers.

7 10, 20, 30, ☐, 50, 60, ☐, 80, …

8 10, ☐, 30, 40, 50, ☐, 70, …

9 10, 20, ☐, 40, 50, 60, 70, ☐, ☐, …

10 50, 60, 70, 80, ☐, ☐, 110, ☐, …

Mark your answers. How well did you do?

Mark ☐ out of 10   Time taken ☐

Write these numbers in words.

1 8

2 2

3 7

4 11

5 12

6 14

7 20

Write these as numbers.

8 nine

9 six

10 thirteen

11 fifteen

12 seventeen

Mark your answers. How well did you do?

Mark ☐ out of 12   Time taken ☐

Test 6: Odd and even

Write **o** for odd or **e** for even to show which each number is.

1 7 ☐   **6** 9 ☐

2 5 ☐   **7** 10 ☐

3 3 ☐   **8** 14 ☐

4 4 ☐   **9** 17 ☐

5 8 ☐   **10** 11 ☐

11 Write an odd number that is greater than 7 and less than 10.   ☐

12 Write an even number that is greater than 10 and less than 13.   ☐

13 Write an even number that is greater than 14 and less than 17.   ☐

14 Write an odd number that is greater than 15 and less than 18.   ☐

Mark your answers. How well did you do?

Mark ☐ out of 14   Time taken ☐

Test 7: One more, one less

What is one more than each number?

1 7 ☐

2 8 ☐

3 19 ☐

4 12 ☐

5 20 ☐

6 26 ☐

7 28 ☐

8 33 ☐

What is one less than each number?

9 14 ☐

10 18 ☐

11 21 ☐

12 29 ☐

13 32 ☐

14 40 ☐

15 60 ☐

16 83 ☐

Mark your answers. How well did you do?

Mark ☐ out of 16   Time taken ☐

Test 8: Adding

How many altogether?

1 3 and 2 is ☐

2 4 and 3 is ☐

3 3 and 5 is ☐

4 4 and 6 is ☐

5 5 and 4 is ☐

Test 9: Addition facts (1)

1 5 + 2 = ☐

2 2 + 2 = ☐

3 2 + 4 = ☐

4 1 + 6 = ☐

5 3 + 4 = ☐

6 2 + 3 = ☐

7 4 + 5 = ☐

8 6 + 2 = ☐

9 3 + 3 = ☐

10 6 + 3 = ☐

11 3 + 5 = ☐

12 5 + 4 = ☐

13 8 + 0 = ☐

14 7 + 2 = ☐

15 4 + 4 = ☐

16 3 + 6 = ☐

Mark your answers. How well did you do?

Mark ☐ out of 16   Time taken ☐

Test 10: Addition facts (2)

Fill in the missing numbers to make 10 each time.

1 $8 + \boxed{} = 10$

2 $7 + \boxed{} = 10$

3 $\boxed{} + 1 = 10$

4 $\boxed{} + 6 = 10$

5 $\boxed{} + 0 = 10$

6 $\boxed{} + 4 = 10$

7 $3 + \boxed{} = 10$

8 $10 + \boxed{} = 10$

9 $\boxed{} + 9 = 10$

10 $\boxed{} + 2 = 10$

11 $4 + \boxed{} = 10$

12 $\boxed{} + 5 = 10$

Mark your answers. How well did you do?

Mark $\boxed{}$ out of 12   Time taken $\boxed{}$

Test 11: Addition facts (3)

1   4 + 7 = ☐

2   5 + 8 = ☐

3   5 + 6 = ☐

4   7 + 6 = ☐

5   6 + 9 = ☐

6   6 + 8 = ☐

7   9 + 2 = ☐

8   3 + 8 = ☐

9   5 + 7 = ☐

10   9 + 4 = ☐

11   7 + 5 = ☐

12   8 + 9 = ☐

13   7 + 8 = ☐

14   5 + 9 = ☐

Mark your answers. How well did you do?

Mark ☐ out of 14   Time taken ☐

Test 12: Mental addition

1 16 + 3 = ☐

2 14 + 2 = ☐

3 13 + 5 = ☐

4 13 + 4 = ☐

5 11 + 6 = ☐

6 12 + 7 = ☐

7 15 + 5 = ☐

8 13 + 6 = ☐

9 11 + 9 = ☐

10 12 + 9 = ☐

11 13 + 8 = ☐

12 15 + 7 = ☐

13 16 + 9 = ☐

14 18 + 7 = ☐

Mark your answers. How well did you do?

Mark ☐ out of 14   Time taken ☐

Test 13: Subtraction facts (1)

1 $9 - 7 = \boxed{}$

2 $8 - 2 = \boxed{}$

3 $7 - 5 = \boxed{}$

4 $8 - 6 = \boxed{}$

5 $9 - 8 = \boxed{}$

6 $7 - 3 = \boxed{}$

7 $9 - 3 = \boxed{}$

8 $8 - 5 = \boxed{}$

9 $7 - 2 = \boxed{}$

10 $6 - 4 = \boxed{}$

11 $5 - 3 = \boxed{}$

12 $8 - 4 = \boxed{}$

13 $8 - 3 = \boxed{}$

14 $9 - 4 = \boxed{}$

15 $7 - 0 = \boxed{}$

16 $9 - 5 = \boxed{}$

Mark your answers. How well did you do?

Mark $\boxed{}$ out of 16   Time taken $\boxed{}$

Test 14: Subtraction facts (2)

1 $10 - \boxed{} = 2$

2 $10 - \boxed{} = 3$

3 $\boxed{} - 3 = 7$

4 $\boxed{} - 5 = 5$

5 $10 - \boxed{} = 4$

6 $10 - \boxed{} = 8$

7 $\boxed{} - 4 = 6$

8 $10 - \boxed{} = 1$

9 $\boxed{} - 0 = 10$

10 $\boxed{} - 7 = 3$

11 $\boxed{} - 1 = 9$

12 $10 - \boxed{} = 5$

13 $\boxed{} - 6 = 4$

14 $\boxed{} - 10 = 0$

Mark your answers. How well did you do?

Mark $\boxed{}$ out of 14   Time taken $\boxed{}$

Test 15: Subtraction facts (3)

1 $13 - 2 = \boxed{}$

2 $14 - 3 = \boxed{}$

3 $13 - 5 = \boxed{}$

4 $12 - 3 = \boxed{}$

5 $19 - 7 = \boxed{}$

6 $18 - 4 = \boxed{}$

7 $11 - 2 = \boxed{}$

8 $16 - 5 = \boxed{}$

9 $11 - 3 = \boxed{}$

10 $20 - 4 = \boxed{}$

11 $17 - 8 = \boxed{}$

12 $18 - 9 = \boxed{}$

13 $14 - 7 = \boxed{}$

14 $12 - 8 = \boxed{}$

Mark your answers. How well did you do?

Mark $\boxed{}$ out of 14   Time taken $\boxed{}$

Test 16: Mental subtraction

0 1 2 3 4 5 6 7 8 9 10 11 12 13 14 15 16 17 18 19 20 21 22 23 24 25

1 $18 - 7 =$ ☐

2 $21 - 2 =$ ☐

3 $16 - 9 =$ ☐

4 $15 - 8 =$ ☐

5 $19 - 9 =$ ☐

6 $20 - 8 =$ ☐

7 $21 - 3 =$ ☐

8 $22 - 5 =$ ☐

9 $18 - 9 =$ ☐

10 $23 - 4 =$ ☐

11 $20 - 7 =$ ☐

12 $21 - 4 =$ ☐

13 $19 - 8 =$ ☐

14 $24 - 6 =$ ☐

Mark your answers. How well did you do?

Mark ☐ out of 14   Time taken ☐

Test 17: Adding three numbers

1 1 + 5 + 2 = ☐

2 2 + 2 + 3 = ☐

3 2 + 1 + 4 = ☐

4 1 + 1 + 6 = ☐

5 3 + 4 + 2 = ☐

6 2 + 3 + 2 = ☐

7 4 + 5 + 1 = ☐

8 6 + 2 + 1 = ☐

9 3 + 3 + 2 = ☐

10 6 + 3 + 2 = ☐

11 3 + 5 + 3 = ☐

12 5 + 4 + 4 = ☐

13 8 + 3 + 1 = ☐

14 7 + 2 + 4 = ☐

15 4 + 4 + 5 = ☐

16 3 + 6 + 7 = ☐

Mark your answers. How well did you do?

Mark ☐ out of 16   Time taken ☐

20

Test 18: Word problems

1 What is 4 plus 2? ☐

2 Add 2 and 7. ☐

3 Take 3 from 6. ☐

4 What is 8 take away 7? ☐

5 What is 9 more than 3? ☐

6 What is the total of 8 and 7? ☐

7 Subtract 5 from 13. ☐

8 What is 12 minus 7? ☐

9 What is 8 less than 22? ☐

10 I have 15 biscuits. 7 get eaten. How many are left? ☐

Mark your answers. How well did you do?

Mark ☐ out of 10   Time taken ☐

Test 19: Doubling

1 2 + 2 = ☐

2 3 + 3 = ☐

3 6 + 6 = ☐

4 5 + 5 = ☐

5 7 + 7 = ☐

6 10 + 10 = ☐

7 4 + 4 = ☐

8 8 + 8 = ☐

9 1 + 1 = ☐

10 9 + 9 = ☐

11 Double 4 is ☐

12 Double 3 is ☐

13 Double 8 is ☐

14 Double 6 is ☐

15 Double 7 is ☐

16 Double 2 is ☐

17 Double 10 is ☐

18 Double 9 is ☐

Mark your answers. How well did you do?

Mark ☐ out of 18   Time taken ☐

Test 20: Early multiplication and division

1 2 + 2 + 2 = ☐

2 3 lots of 2 is ☐

3 How many stars are there? 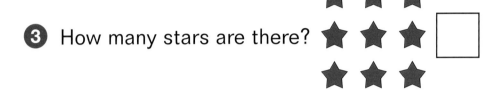 ☐

4 What is 2 lots of 5? ☐

5 3 + 3 + 3 + 3 = ☐

6 4 × 3 = ☐

7 What is 6 shared equally between 2? ☐

8 What is half of 10? ☐

9 Split 9 into groups of 3. How many groups are there? ☐

10 15 ÷ 3 = ☐

Mark your answers. How well did you do?

Mark ☐ out of 10   Time taken ☐

Colour $\frac{1}{2}$ of each shape.

1

2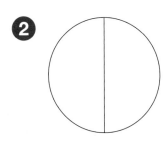

3

4

5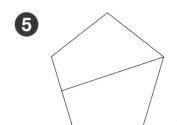

6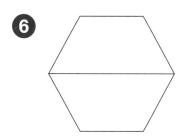

7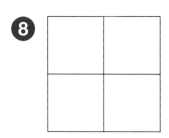

8

Mark your answers. How well did you do?

Mark ☐ out of 8   Time taken ☐

Ring $\frac{1}{2}$ of the sweets in each set.

1

4

2

5

3

6
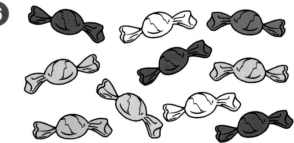

Mark your answers. How well did you do?

Mark ☐ out of 6   Time taken ☐

1 Half of 4 is ☐

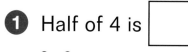

4 Half of 6 is ☐

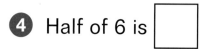

2 Half of 12 is ☐

5 Half of 16 is ☐

3 Half of 2 is ☐

6 Half of 14 is ☐

7 $\frac{1}{2}$ of 10 = ☐

9 $\frac{1}{2}$ of 8 = ☐

8 $\frac{1}{2}$ of 20 = ☐

10 $\frac{1}{2}$ of 100 = ☐

Mark your answers. How well did you do?

Mark ☐ out of 10   Time taken ☐

1 Colour $\frac{1}{4}$ of this shape.

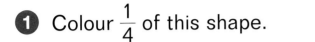

2 Colour $\frac{1}{4}$ of this shape.

3 Colour $\frac{3}{4}$ of this shape.

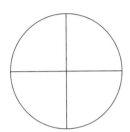

4 Colour $\frac{3}{4}$ of this shape.

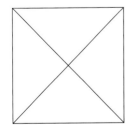

5 Colour $\frac{1}{4}$ of this shape.

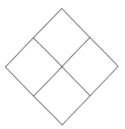

6 Colour $\frac{3}{4}$ of this shape.

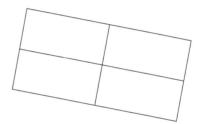

7 Colour $\frac{3}{4}$ of this shape.

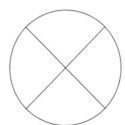

8 Colour $\frac{1}{4}$ of this shape.

Mark your answers. How well did you do?

Mark ☐ out of 8   Time taken ☐

Ring $\frac{1}{4}$ of the sweets in each set.

1

3

2

4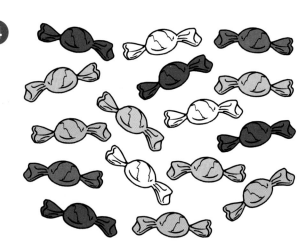

Ring $\frac{3}{4}$ of the sweets in each set.

5

6

Mark your answers. How well did you do?

Mark ☐ out of 6   Time taken ☐

Write what fraction of each shape is shaded.

1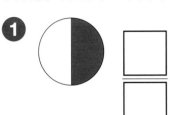

6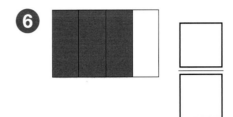

2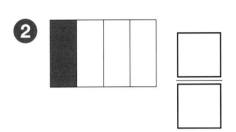

7

3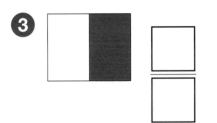

8

4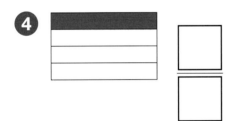

9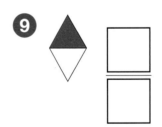

5

10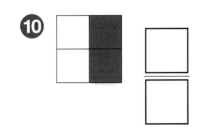

Mark your answers. How well did you do?

Mark ☐ out of 10   Time taken ☐

1 One quarter of 4 is ☐

2 Half of 6 is ☐

3 One quarter of 8 is ☐

4 Three quarters of 4 is ☐

5 Three quarters of 8 is ☐

6 Three quarters of 20 is ☐

7 $\frac{1}{4}$ of 12 = ☐

8 $\frac{1}{4}$ of 16 = ☐

9 $\frac{1}{2}$ of 40 = ☐

10 $\frac{3}{4}$ of 12 = ☐

Mark your answers. How well did you do?

Mark ☐ out of 10   Time taken ☐

Use the words in the box to name each shape.

| circle | triangle | square | rectangle |

1

5

2

6

3

7

4

8

Mark your answers. How well did you do?

Mark ⬚ out of 8   Time taken ⬚

Test 29: 3D shapes

Use the words in the box to name the shape shown in each picture.

pyramid   cone   cube   sphere

1

5

2

6

3

7

4

8

Mark your answers. How well did you do?

Mark [ ] out of 8   Time taken [   ]

Test 30: Position

Cat	Fox	Hat
Cup	Sock	Ball
Tree	Shoe	Fly

What is:

1 next to the ball?

2 above the sock?

3 under the cat?

4 between the tree and the fly?

5 left of the fox?

6 right of the shoe?

7 beside the tree?

8 beneath the hat?

Mark your answers. How well did you do?

Mark ☐ out of 8   Time taken

Test 31: Turns

Tick to show whether the hand is turned through a quarter turn or a half turn to make the second print.

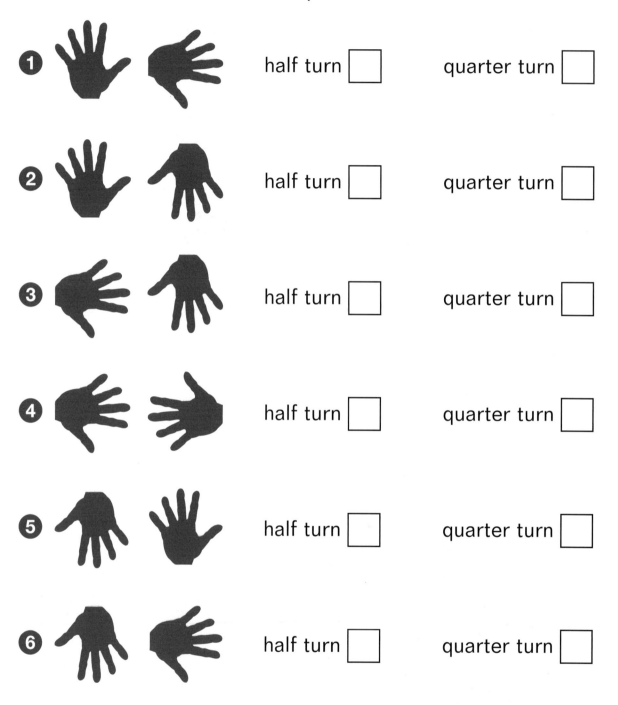

1   half turn ☐   quarter turn ☐

2   half turn ☐   quarter turn ☐

3   half turn ☐   quarter turn ☐

4   half turn ☐   quarter turn ☐

5   half turn ☐   quarter turn ☐

6   half turn ☐   quarter turn ☐

Mark your answers. How well did you do?

Mark ☐ out of 6   Time taken ☐

Test 32: Comparing lengths

Tick which is longer in each pair.

1

2

3

4

5

6

Mark your answers. How well did you do?

Mark [ ] out of 6   Time taken [ ]

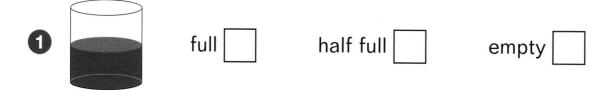

Tick to show how full each pot is.

1   full ☐   half full ☐   empty ☐

2   full ☐   half full ☐   empty ☐

3   full ☐   half full ☐   empty ☐

4   full ☐   half full ☐   empty ☐

Colour so that the pot is:

5 half full

7 full

6 quarter full

8 three-quarters full

Mark your answers. How well did you do?

Mark ☐ out of 8   Time taken ☐

Test 34: Units

Draw a line to match each unit with the missing measurement in each set.

1 A worm is ☐ long   10 kilograms

A TV weighs ☐   10 centimetres

A bucket holds ☐ of water   10 litres

2 My road is ☐ long   100 grams

I drank ☐ of juice   100 millilitres

A glass weighs ☐   100 metres

3 A tomato weighs ☐   50 centimetres

A bath holds ☐ of water   50 litres

My TV is ☐ tall   50 grams

Mark your answers. How well did you do?

Mark ☐ out of 9   Time taken ▭

Test 35: Telling time – analogue (1)

Write these times using the words '**half past**' and '**o'clock**'.

1

2

3

4

5

6

7

8

9

10

Mark your answers. How well did you do?

Mark ☐ out of 10   Time taken ☐

Draw hands on the clocks to show these times.

1 half-past two

5 half-past six

2 seven o'clock

6 eleven o'clock

3 half-past four

7 six o'clock

4 nine o'clock

8 half-past five

Mark your answers. How well did you do?

Mark ☐ out of 8   Time taken ☐

Test 37: Coins

Write the value of each coin.

1 ☐

5  ☐

2  ☐

6  ☐

3  ☐

7  ☐

4  ☐

8  ☐

Mark your answers. How well did you do?

Mark ☐ out of 8   Time taken ☐

Test 38: Days of the week

Use the words in the box to help you answer the questions.

Monday	Tuesday	Wednesday	Thursday
	Friday	Saturday	Sunday	

1 The day after Monday is [_____].

2 The day after Friday is [_____].

3 The day after Sunday is [_____].

4 The day after Tuesday is [_____].

5 The day before Sunday is [_____].

6 The day before Monday is [_____].

7 The day before Friday is [_____].

8 The day before Tuesday is [_____].

Mark your answers. How well did you do?

Mark [____] out of 8   Time taken [_____]

Answers

Test 1
1 The team with 4 children.
2 The team with 6 children.
3 The team with 7 children.
4 The bowl with 3 apples.
5 The bowl with 4 apples.
6 The bowl with 6 apples.

Test 2
1 3
2 5
3 7
4 9
5 6
6 2, 4, 5, 8
7 2, 6, 7, 11
8 1, 6, 9, 12
9 13, 14, 15, 18

Test 3
1 5
2 9
3 15
4 18
5 17, 18, 19
6 35, 36, 37
7 99, 100, 101
8 79, 78, 77
9 60, 59, 58
10 96, 95, 94

Test 4
1 8, 14
2 4, 16
3 16, 18, 24
4 25, 45

5 10, 40
6 45, 50, 60
7 40, 70
8 20, 60
9 30, 80, 90
10 90, 100, 120

Test 5
1 eight
2 two
3 seven
4 eleven
5 twelve
6 fourteen
7 twenty
8 9
9 6
10 13
11 15
12 17

Test 6
1 o
2 o
3 o
4 e
5 e
6 o
7 e
8 e
9 o
10 o
11 9
12 12
13 16
14 17

Test 7

1 8
2 9
3 20
4 13
5 21
6 27
7 29
8 34
9 13
10 17
11 20
12 28
13 31
14 39
15 59
16 82

Test 8

1 5
2 7
3 8
4 10
5 9

Test 9

1 7
2 4
3 6
4 7
5 7
6 5
7 9
8 8
9 6
10 9

11 8
12 9
13 8
14 9
15 8
16 9

Test 10

1 2
2 3
3 9
4 4
5 10
6 6
7 7
8 0
9 1
10 8
11 6
12 5

Test 11

1 11
2 13
3 11
4 13
5 15
6 14
7 11
8 11
9 12
10 13
11 12
12 17
13 15
14 14

Test 12

1 19
2 16
3 18
4 17
5 17
6 19
7 20
8 19
9 20
10 21
11 21
12 22
13 25
14 25

Test 13

1 2
2 6
3 2
4 2
5 1
6 4
7 6
8 3
9 5
10 2
11 2
12 4
13 5
14 5
15 7
16 4

Test 14

1 8

2 7
3 10
4 10
5 6
6 2
7 10
8 9
9 10
10 10
11 10
12 5
13 10
14 10

Test 15

1 11
2 11
3 8
4 9
5 12
6 14
7 9
8 11
9 8
10 16
11 9
12 9
13 7
14 4

Test 16

1 11
2 19
3 7
4 7
5 10

6 12
7 18
8 17
9 9
10 19
11 13
12 17
13 11
14 18

Test 17
1 8
2 7
3 7
4 8
5 9
6 7
7 10
8 9
9 8
10 11
11 11
12 13
13 12
14 13
15 13
16 16

Test 18
1 6
2 9
3 3
4 1
5 12
6 15
7 8

8 5
9 14
10 8

Test 19
1 4
2 6
3 12
4 10
5 14
6 20
7 8
8 16
9 2
10 18
11 8
12 6
13 16
14 12
15 14
16 4
17 20
18 18

Test 20
1 6
2 6
3 9
4 10
5 12
6 12
7 3 each
8 5
9 3
10 5

Test 21
Half of each shape should be coloured.

Test 22
1 2 sweets should be circled.
2 3 sweets should be circled.
3 1 sweet should be circled.
4 4 sweets should be circled.
5 6 sweets should be circled.
6 5 sweets should be circled.

Test 23
1 2
2 6
3 1
4 3
5 8
6 7
7 5
8 10
9 4
10 50

Test 24
One quarter or three quarters of each shape should be shaded.

Test 25
1 1 sweet should be circled.
2 2 sweets should be circled.
3 3 sweets should be circled.
4 4 sweets should be circled.
5 3 sweets should be circled.
6 6 sweets should be circled.

Test 26
1 $\frac{1}{2}$
2 $\frac{1}{4}$
3 $\frac{1}{2}$
4 $\frac{1}{4}$
5 $\frac{1}{2}$
6 $\frac{3}{4}$
7 $\frac{1}{4}$
8 $\frac{3}{4}$
9 $\frac{1}{2}$
10 $\frac{1}{2}$ or $\frac{2}{4}$

Test 27
1 1
2 3
3 2
4 3
5 6
6 15
7 3
8 4
9 20
10 9

Test 28
1 rectangle
2 circle
3 square
4 triangle
5 square
6 triangle
7 rectangle
8 triangle

Test 29
1 pyramid
2 sphere
3 cone
4 cube
5 cube
6 cone
7 pyramid
8 sphere

Test 30
1 sock or hat or fly
2 fox
3 cup
4 shoe
5 cat
6 fly
7 shoe
8 ball

Test 31
1 quarter turn
2 half turn
3 quarter turn
4 half turn
5 half turn
6 quarter turn

Test 32
The longer item should be marked each time.

Test 33
1 half full
2 full
3 empty
4 half full
5 The pot coloured half full.
6 The pot coloured a quarter full.
7 The pot coloured full.
8 The pot coloured three-quarters full.

Test 34
1 10 centimetres
10 kilograms
10 litres
2 100 metres
100 millilitres
100 grams
3 50 grams
50 litres
50 centimetres

Test 35
1 5 o'clock
2 7 o'clock
3 half past 2
4 half past 8
5 11 o'clock
6 half past 1
7 half past 12
8 6 o'clock
9 half past 10
10 half past 6

Test 36

1

2

3

4

5

6

7

8

Test 37

1 5p

2 10p

3 2p

4 20p

5 1p

6 50p

7 £1

8 £2

Test 38

1 Tuesday

2 Saturday

3 Monday

4 Wednesday

5 Saturday

6 Sunday

7 Thursday

8 Monday